African Americans Today

Stephanie Kuligowski, M.A.T.

D0770329

Consultant

Marcus McArthur, Ph.D.
Department of History
Saint Louis University

Publishing Credits

Dona Herweck Rice, *Editor-in-Chief*
Lee Aucoin, *Creative Director*
Chris McIntyre, M.A.Ed., *Editorial Director*
Torrey Maloof, *Associate Editor*
Neri Garcia, *Senior Designer*
Stephanie Reid, *Photo Researcher*
Rachelle Cracchiolo, M.S.Ed., *Publisher*

Image Credits

cover Newscom; p.1 Newscom; p.4 (top) The Library of Congress; p.4 (bottom) The Library of Congress; p.5 (left) The Library of Congress; p.5 (right) Shutterstock, Inc.; p.6 (top, left) Getty Images; p.6 (top, right) Corbis; p.6 (bottom) The Library of Congress; p.7 The Library of Congress; p.8 Corbis; p.9 (top) Getty Images; p.9 (bottom) Shutterstock, Inc.; p.10 (top) The Library of Congress; p.10 (bottom) United States Defense Department; p.11 Getty Images; p.12 National Aeronautics and Space Administration; p.13 (left) United States Patent and Trademark Office; p.13 (right) Newscom.; p.14 Stephen Parker/Alamy; p.15 Getty Images; p.16 Newscom; p.17 Newscom; p.18 (top) Getty Images; p.18 (bottom) Getty Images; p.19 Rex, USA; p.20 (top) Shutterstock, Inc.; p.20 (bottom) Getty Images; p.21 (top) Getty Images; p.21 (bottom) Shutterstock, Inc.; p.22 (top, left) Shutterstock, Inc.; p.22 (top, right) Shutterstock, Inc.; p.22 (bottom) Shutterstock, Inc.; p.23 Daily Mail/Rex/Alamy; p.24 Pictorial Press Ltd./Alamy; p.25 (top) Getty Images; p.25 (bottom) Getty Images; p.26 Getty Images; p.27 (top) Mark Downey/Alamy; p.27 (bottom) Getty Images; p.29 (left) Getty Images; p.29 (right) Newscom.; p.32 (left) Shutterstock, Inc.; p.32 (right) Getty Images

Teacher Created Materials

5301 Oceanus Drive
Huntington Beach, CA 92649-1030
http://www.tcmpub.com
ISBN 978-1-4333-1688-3

Copyright © 2012 by Teacher Created Materials, Inc.
Made in China
YiCai.032019.CA201901471

Table of Contents

Those Who Overcame

Not long ago in the United States, African Americans had to live by different rules than other people. They were **segregated**. This means that they were separated from white people. They could not share restrooms, drinking fountains, or parks. They had to sit in the backs of buses and movie theaters.

The Civil Rights Movement of the 1950s and 1960s, led by Dr. Martin Luther King Jr., helped put an end to segregation. But many people held onto their **prejudices** (PREJ-uh-dis-iz) against African Americans. A prejudice is an unfair opinion formed without facts or evidence. Prejudices put African Americans at a disadvantage.

Segregated drinking fountain

March on Washington for Civil Rights in 1963

Dr. Martin Luther King Jr.

Oprah Winfrey

Separate but Equal?

In 1954, the United States Supreme Court ruled that "separate but equal" laws were unfair. The schools, restrooms, and parks for African Americans were almost always older and more rundown than those for white people. America finally began to **integrate**, or bring the races together.

America's Early Promise

America's founding fathers defined the newly free country of the United States of America with these words: *"We hold these truths to be self-evident, that all men are created equal, that they are endowed by their Creator with certain unalienable Rights, that among these are Life, Liberty, and the Pursuit of Happiness."*

The people in this book have overcome those disadvantages. Oprah Winfrey has reigned over the entertainment world with her own talk show, television network, movie studio, and magazine. Colin Powell became the first African American secretary of state. Maya Angelou (AN-juh-loo) was asked to write a poem for the president's **inauguration** (in-aw-gyuh-REY-shuhn). And, Muhammad Ali was the heavyweight boxing champion of the world.

These Americans dreamed big. They practiced, studied, and trained. They never took no for an answer. They climbed to the top of their chosen fields. And by doing so, they cut paths for others to follow.

Quotas

In the 1970s, some whites began to complain that affirmative action was "reverse discrimination." They said that African Americans were given unfair advantages. Many people objected to the use of **quotas** in hiring and school admissions. A quota is a minimum number of minority employees or students set by a business or school.

Tested in the Courts

From the 1970s until today, affirmative action policies have been challenged in the courts. Some policies were found to be unconstitutional. Others were allowed to stand.

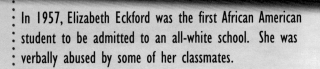

In 1957, Elizabeth Eckford was the first African American student to be admitted to an all-white school. She was verbally abused by some of her classmates.

President Johnson signs the Civil Rights Act.

Equal Opportunities

In 1961, President John F. Kennedy asked American schools and businesses to take **affirmative action**. He wanted African Americans to have equal opportunities in education and employment. He issued an executive order. It required programs using federal money to be free from prejudice. Kennedy also set up the Committee on Equal Employment Opportunities.

The years after Kennedy's order were the most violent of the Civil Rights Movement. In the South, **discrimination** and violence against African Americans continued. African Americans fought back. Then Congress passed the Civil Rights Act in 1964. This banned discrimination based on color, race, religion, or national origin.

President Kennedy

Still, equality for all Americans would not happen overnight. In 1965, President Lyndon B. Johnson noted that civil rights laws alone would not correct the inequalities in America. He explained that affirmative action was the next step in the fight for civil rights.

Later that same year, Johnson issued an executive order to enforce affirmative action. Companies working with the government would have to hire and promote **minority** employees. And, the government would check on their efforts.

Striving for Success

Soldier at Heart: Colin Powell

General Colin Powell never wanted to be fourth in line to the presidency. He did not want to travel the world as a **diplomat** (DIP-luh-mat). He did not want to write reports and make speeches. He wanted to be a soldier.

Powell was a boy during World War II and the Korean War. He loved hearing war stories. He and his neighborhood friends in the Bronx played with toy soldiers and fought imaginary battles.

When Powell went to college, he joined the campus military training program. After college, he joined the army. He loved the order and structure of military life. He rose through the ranks to become a four-star general in command of a million soldiers. He was then named chairman of the Joint Chiefs of Staff. Powell was now the top military officer in the country.

Powell joined the Reserve Officers' Training Corps (ROTC) when he was 17 years old.

General Colin Powell shakes hands with crew members of a battleship during the Persian Gulf War.

Changing the Laws

As an African American lawyer in the 1950s, Thurgood Marshall worked to end segregation. He won the *Brown v. Board of Education* case in 1954. That victory ended legal segregation in public schools. He successfully challenged many other "separate but equal" laws. In 1967, he became the first African American justice on the United States Supreme Court.

Famous First

Barack Obama was born in Hawaii in 1961. His mother was a white woman from Kansas and his father was a black man from Africa. Having one white parent and one black parent helped Obama understand the issues of race in America. Obama used that understanding as a lawyer and community organizer. In 2004, he was elected to the United States Senate. In 2008, Obama became the first African American president of the United States.

Secretary of State Colin Powell

Powell was a brave, honorable, and wise soldier. Those qualities caught the attention of America's most powerful people. The president and others asked him to take leadership roles in government. Powell said no many times. But he finally agreed to trade his uniform for a suit. He became the first African American secretary of state in 2001.

: Shirley Chisholm

A Voice for Change

Shirley Chisholm was a New York City educator. She saw firsthand the problems of children, women, and minorities in her part of the city. In the 1950s, she decided she wanted to speak for these people in government. She won a seat in the New York State legislature in 1964 and the United States Congress in 1968. She was the first African American woman elected to the U.S. Congress. In 1972, Chisholm became the first woman and first African American to run for president for a major party.

Madam Senator

In 1992, Carol Moseley-Braun of Illinois became the first African American woman to serve in the United States Senate.

Reaching for the Top: Condoleezza Rice

Condoleezza Rice was born in 1954 in Birmingham, Alabama. It was not the easiest time or place to be an African American. But the racism Rice faced did not hold her back. It gave her a motive to work harder.

Rice was a top student. She was so bright that she skipped the first and seventh grades. She graduated from high school at 16 and went on to college. She studied world relations and became a professor.

: Secretary of State Condoleezza Rice

Rice's area of **expertise** (ek-sper-TEEZ) was the Soviet Union. It was a large country that was often at odds with the United States. In the late 1980s, the government of the Soviet Union fell apart. President George H. W. Bush needed advice from people who understood the country. Rice moved to Washington, DC, to help.

President Bush and Rice worked closely together for many years.

George H. W. Bush's son, George W. Bush, ran for president in 2000. Rice advised him on international relations. When he won the election, he gave Rice the job of national security advisor. She was the first woman to have that job.

Bush was reelected in 2004. He made Rice secretary of state. She became the nation's top diplomat. Her years of hard work had led her to the White House.

Science Pioneers

Guion (GUY-un) "Guy" Bluford and Patricia Bath are modern **pioneers**.

A high school counselor told Bluford that he was not "college material." But, he earned a college degree in **aerospace engineering**. He then joined the United States Air Force. He also served as a pilot in the Vietnam War.

After earning top degrees, Bluford applied to become an astronaut at the National Aeronautics and Space Administration (NASA). Bluford was chosen out of 10,000 people who applied. In 1979, Bluford became the first African American astronaut. He was the first African American to travel in space.

Bluford runs on a treadmill in space.

United States Patent [19]
th

[11] Patent Number: 5,919,186
[45] Date of Patent: *Jul. 6, 1999

LASER APPARATUS FOR SURGERY OF
CATARACTOUS LENSES

Inventor: Patricia E. Bath, 4554 Circle View
Blvd., Los Angeles, Calif. 90043

Notice: This patent is subject to a terminal dis-
claimer.

Appl. No.: 08/854,138

Filed: May 8, 1997

Related U.S. Application Data

Continuation of application No. 07/717,794, Jun. 19, 1991,
which is a continuation of application No. 07/159,931, Feb.
24, 1988, which is a division of application No. 06/943,098,
Dec. 18, 1986, Pat. No. 4,744,360.

Int. Cl.⁶ A61N 5/06
U.S. Cl. 606/6; 606/3; 606/10;
606/15
Field of Search 606/3–6, 10–18

References Cited
U.S. PATENT DOCUMENTS

3,433,226 3/1969 Boyd .
3,971,383 7/1976 Krasnov .
3,982,541 9/1976 L'Esperance, Jr. .
4,320,761 3/1982 Haddad 604/22
4,538,608 9/1985 L'Esperance 606/5

4,583,539 4/1986 Karlin et al. 606/4
4,686,979 8/1987 Gruen et al. .
4,694,828 9/1987 Eichenbaum 606/6
4,744,360 5/1988 Bath .
5,324,282 6/1994 Dodick .
5,334,183 8/1994 Wuchinich .

OTHER PUBLICATIONS

C. Davis Belcher III, "The Future", Ophthalmic Laser
Therapy, vol. 2, No. 4, 1987
C. Davis Belcher III, "Phacoablation", Ophthalmic Laser
Therapy, vol. 3, No. 1, 1988.
Gailitis   et   al.,   "Comparison   of   Laser
Phacovaporization . . . ", '78/SPIE vol. 1744, Ophthalmic
Technologies II (1992).

Primary Examiner—David M. Shay

[57]   ABSTRACT

A method and apparatus for removing cataracts in which a
flexible line preferably 1 mm or less in diameter is inserted
through an incision into the anterior chamber until its end is
adjacent the cataract. Coherent radiation, preferably at a
frequency between 193 and 351 nm, is coupled to the
cataract by an optical fiber in the line. An irrigation sleeve
provided about the fiber and an aspiration sleeve extending
partially around the irrigation sleeve conduct irrigating
liquid to and remove ablated material from the anterior
chamber and form with the optical fiber the flexible line.

17 Claims, 1 Drawing Sheet

This is the patent for Bath's invention.

Helping Others

Bath's research showed that African Americans were twice as likely to go blind and six times more likely to get the eye disease glaucoma (glaw-KOH-muh) than people of other races. To help correct this, Bath set up a system to provide eye care to people who could not afford it.

Computer Whiz

Computer engineer Mark Dean made it possible to plug printers, disc drives, and monitors directly into computers. He also helped develop the color PC monitor and the first gigahertz chip. This chip could make a billion calculations per second. Dean holds more than 20 patents for his inventions.

Patricia Bath was a bright student. She had a strong interest in science. She graduated from high school in just two years! She went to college and then medical school. She became a doctor of **ophthalmology** (op-thuhl-MOL-uh-jee) in 1968. This branch of medicine focuses on eye diseases. Bath became the first African American in that field.

Bath invented a special probe to help treat eye problems. With her invention, Bath was able to restore sight to many people who had been blind for years. Bath got a **patent** for her invention in 1988.

Writing from Experience

Women Writers

Maya Angelou and Toni Morrison are two of the most important writers in America today. They both also happen to be African American women.

Maya Angelou grew up in segregated Stamps, Arkansas, in the 1930s. To support herself and her son, she worked as a waitress, a fry cook, a trolley conductor, and a nightclub singer. She was even an actress in a play and toured the world!

When Angelou returned home, she wrote an autobiography about her unusual life. It became a bestseller. The next year, her first book of poetry was nominated for a **Pulitzer Prize**.

: Maya Angelou

Poem for the President

In 1992, President Bill Clinton asked Maya Angelou to write a poem for his inauguration ceremony. She was the first African American and the first woman to write a poem for a president.

Famous First

Alice Walker became the first African American woman to win the Pulitzer Prize for fiction in 1983. She won the award for her novel *The Color Purple*.

Toni Morrison was born poor, female, and African American in 1931. At that time, those qualities were disadvantages. But Morrison's parents expected great things from their children. They worked hard and saved money to send them to college. Morrison became a college professor and then a book editor.

In 1970, Morrison published her first novel, *The Bluest Eye*. Her fifth book, *Beloved*, is about the painful subject of slavery. Critics called the book one of the greatest American novels ever written. It won the Pulitzer Prize for fiction. In 1993, Morrison became the first African American winner of the **Nobel Prize** for literature. This award is the world's top honor for writers.

Toni Morrison

The Power of His Pen

Leonard Pitts Jr. pays attention to world events. He then forms opinions and writes them down. He is a newspaper **columnist** (KOL-uhm-nist). His column is published twice a week in many American newspapers. Millions of people want to read what Pitts thinks about life.

Pitts started his career as an 18-year-old college student. He wrote for *SOUL*, an African American entertainment magazine. Two years later, he became the magazine's editor. His writing has been published in national magazines from *TV Guide* to *Parenting*. He has also written several books.

Words have power, and Pitts knows how to wield that power. Sometimes he writes about **pop culture**. Sometimes he writes about politics. Sometimes he writes about family life. For every topic, Pitts uses words to open minds and touch hearts.

Leonard Pitts Jr.

The newspaper clipping (a photograph of a printed page):

The newspaper clip text (readable portions):

REMEMBER
September 11, 2001

A nation united

Immediately after the terrorist attacks, Leonard Pitts' words struck a chord with the nation.
Now, one year later, he again reflects on America's reaction to our national tragedy.

'We've learned that we can no longer escape who we are'

LEONARD
PITTS JR.
Knight Ridder
Newspapers

'We will rise in defense of all that we cherish'

"We're being hijacked! We're being hijacked!"
— Passenger aboard United Airlines Flight 93, screaming into a cell phone as the plane went down, Sept. 11, 2001

"We're in the World Trade Center and it has just been bombed. We are OK, but I think a lot of people are dead."
— Bob Hurley, of Atlanta, speaking to a reporter by cell phone, Sept. 11, 2001. Hurley, who was on the 22nd floor, survived

"Everyone was screaming, crying, running. Cops, people, firefighters, everyone. It's like a war zone."
— Mike Smith, New York City fire marshal, Sept. 11, 2001

"I can't believe what I'm seeing. I never thought I would see anything like this in my lifetime. How can we stop something like this from happening?"
— Beverly Evans, 20, of Dallas, Sept. 11, 2001

"When I saw the second plane, it seemed like it was flying low. The next thing I see is flames. ... I couldn't believe it was happening. It was like in the movies. I couldn't hear anything, but maybe I couldn't hear anything because I was in such shock."
— Andrea Louie, Brooklyn, N.Y.

"We are at war, we are actually at war. This is a 21st-century war."
— U.S. Rep. Curt Weldon, R-Pa., Sept. 11, 2001

KRT 9/11 ANNIVERSARY SECTION, PAGE 9 OF 12
KNIGHT RIDDER/TRIBUNE

Pitt's wrote a very famous column about the September 11, 2001 terrorist attacks.

A Letter to Terrorists

Pitts used his special talent with words following the September 11, 2001 terrorist attacks on America. Pitts's column was an angry letter to the terrorists. The title was "We'll Go Forward from This Moment." Readers were deeply moved. The piece was emailed to thousands of people around the world. The words were turned into a song and printed on posters.

That Is a Lot of Readers!

Millions of people read Pitts's columns. They are published in over 200 newspapers. Every time a new column is published, Pitts receives almost 2,500 emails from his readers.

In 2004, Pitts won the Pulitzer Prize for **commentary**. That is the highest honor in his field. Pitts also teaches college journalism classes and writes novels.

17

Loving and Strict

Oprah Winfrey was born on a farm in Mississippi in 1954. Her parents were very young, so they left their little girl in the care of her grandma. Her grandma was loving but also strict. She taught Winfrey to read, write, add, and subtract by the age of 3!

Quite a Club!

Winfrey loves books. She loved reading books when she was a young girl, and books still hold a special place in her heart today. In 1996, Winfrey decided she wanted to share her love of books. She started a feature on her show called Oprah's Book Club. When Winfrey selected a book for the club, it became very popular. Sometimes millions of copies sold because Winfrey had picked it for her club!

Winfrey interviewing First Lady Laura Bush on her talk show

Winfrey and Barack Obama during his run for the presidency

Entertaining the Masses

Queen of Daytime Television

Oprah Winfrey hosted her own daytime talk show for more than 25 years. Her fans felt like she was a friend. After all, viewers had seen Winfrey laugh, cry, and open her heart on camera for years.

Winfrey's style of interviewing had always set her apart. As a young TV newscaster, Winfrey had trouble hiding her emotions. Reporters are supposed to be **impartial** (im-PAHR-shuhl), or neutral. They should not give their own thoughts and feelings on a matter. Her boss did not know what to do with a newscaster who cried during interviews! So, he made her the host of a new local talk show. It was first called *AM Chicago*. It was later renamed *The Oprah Winfrey Show*.

The Oprah Winfrey Show was a huge hit. And, it was a perfect fit for Winfrey. Within 10 years, Winfrey's show was broadcast across the country. She won many awards. She became the first African American billionaire. Winfrey likes to share her money with needy people. She has given more than $50 million to charity.

Winfrey's show focused on helping people live their best lives. She says, "It doesn't matter who you are, where you come from. The ability to triumph begins with you. Always."

Winfrey in high school

A Prince from Philly

Before he was a movie star, Will Smith was known as the Fresh Prince. That was the name he used as a rapper when he first came to Hollywood. Smith was only 18 years old then. He and a friend had formed a rap group while in high school in Philadelphia.

The two young men got a record deal. They released their first song a few weeks before graduation! The duo's music focused on middle-class African American life. Smith refused to use swear words in his songs because he wanted to make his family proud.

In 1990, Smith got the lead role in the television show, *The Fresh Prince of Bel Air*. He played the Fresh Prince for six years before turning his focus to movies. Smith continues to work as both a rapper and an actor. In 2002, he was nominated for an **Academy Award** for his role as boxer Muhammad Ali. He did not win the award, but people took notice of his serious acting talent.

Actor Will Smith

Smith's rap group was called D. J. Jazzy Jeff and the Fresh Prince.

Actor James
Earl Jones

Luke, I Am Your Father

James Earl Jones has one of the most recognizable voices in show business. His powerful vocal chords made Darth Vader a memorable villain in the first three *Star Wars* movies. And he was the voice of Mufasa in *The Lion King*. During his long acting career, he has played many characters on stage and screen. He has won many awards and was nominated for an Academy Award.

Blues Man

B.B. King is known as one of the greatest guitarists of all time. As a boy in Mississippi in the 1930s, he grew up singing **gospel music** in church and singing the blues while working in cotton fields. He bought his first guitar at age 12. In 1949, he began recording blues albums. He has won many awards. In 1987, he was inducted into the Rock and Roll Hall of Fame.

Musician B. B. King

Lisa Leslie

Slam Dunk

Lisa Leslie dominated the sport of women's basketball for many years. She played in the Women's National Basketball Association (WNBA) since the league's first year. In 11 seasons with the Los Angeles Sparks, she led the team to two WNBA championships. She won four gold medals as a member of the United States Olympic basketball team. She was also the first woman to dunk the ball in a professional basketball game.

Gold Medal Gymnast

Dominique Dawes was a member of the United States Olympic gymnastics team. She was the first African American woman to win an individual Olympic medal in artistic gymnastics.

Venus Williams

Serena Williams

Sports Superstars

Grand Slam Sisters

Sisters Venus and Serena Williams have dominated women's tennis for more than a decade. Both women's serves have been clocked at over 100 miles per hour. Their strength and speed have changed the sport. All players must now be stronger and faster to keep up.

The story of their lives is unique. Before the girls were born, their father knew he wanted to raise tennis players. He studied the sport by watching matches on television. He rented how-to videos and read books. When the girls turned four years old, he started teaching them.

Venus and Serena lived in a rough neighborhood near Los Angeles in California. They started their daily practices by sweeping litter off the courts. But, that did not keep the Williams family from dreaming big.

The girls loved the sport. Their father's dream became their own, and they have worked hard to make it come true. Venus and Serena have each earned the rank of number-one female tennis player in the world. They also won Olympic gold medals for doubles tennis.

The Williams sisters (Venus and Serena)

The Greatest of All Time

A young boxer named Cassius Clay told the world that he would be the greatest of all time. And, he made good on his promise. In 1961 at the age of 18, he won the Olympic gold medal for boxing. In 1964, he became the heavyweight champion of the world.

Boxing fans were wowed by Clay's talent. He was strong and quick. But he was also as graceful as a dancer. Before his match for the heavyweight world championship, he taunted his opponent with a now-famous rhyme. "Float like a butterfly, sting like a bee, you can't hit what you can't see."

His boastful poetry made Clay a household name in America. His big personality made boxing more popular than ever.

In 1963, Clay changed his name to Muhammad Ali after converting to the religion of Islam. He continued to box until 1981. Throughout his life, Ali has fought for civil rights. In 2005, he was honored with the Presidential Medal of Freedom for his efforts.

Boxer Muhammad Ali

A Winning Career

Former National Football League (NFL) coach Tony Dungy was the first African American to lead a team to a Super Bowl victory. As head coach of the Indianapolis Colts, he made history in 2007 when his team won the NFL championship game. Dungy also was the first head coach to beat all 32 NFL teams. In his last 10 seasons as a head coach, his teams made the playoffs every year.

Indianapolis Colts Coach Tony Dungy

Michael Jordan flies through the air.

Air Jordan

Michael Jordan is one of the greatest basketball players of all time. He had an unmatched combination of athleticism, speed, grace, and acrobatics. Basketball fans remember the icon seemingly flying through the air en route to a slam dunk. He led the Chicago Bulls to six championships in the 1990s. He was chosen as the league's MVP, or most valuable player, five times.

A firefighter battles fires caused by the rioting in Los Angeles.

Damage Report

President George H. W. Bush had to send troops to the city of Los Angeles to help control the riots. By the time they restored order, 55 people were dead, 2,000 were hurt, and nearly 4,000 buildings were burned. The Los Angeles Riots of 1992 were the most destructive racial incident of the twentieth century.

A Second Trial

In 1993, the four police officers were charged in federal court for violating Rodney King's constitutional rights. Two of the officers were found guilty and sent to prison.

Tensions Erupt

By the 1990s, African Americans had won many battles for equal rights. Segregation had ended. African Americans had made names for themselves in politics, science, literature, entertainment, and sports. Despite this progress, racial tension still lay beneath the surface.

In 1992, that tension erupted like a volcano. It spewed violence that took federal troops days to end. African Americans in Los Angeles, California, **rioted** to protest a court ruling.

One year before the riots, an African American named Rodney King led police on a high-speed chase. King finally surrendered. Video filmed by a bystander seemed to show that King was uncooperative and that three white police officers beat him. When the video was broadcast, people were outraged. The three officers and their commander were arrested.

The case went to trial. The jury, which had no African American members, found the police officers not guilty. This angered some residents of Los Angeles and riots broke out. The violence lasted for days.

Many stores and buildings in Los Angeles were destroyed during the riots.

President Bush toured the city of Los Angeles following the riots.

Another March on Washington

In the years following the Los Angeles riots, African Americans continued to face challenges. The **unemployment** rates of African Americans were twice as high as those of whites. And, nearly 40 percent of African Americans were living in **poverty**.

In 1995, a group of African American leaders began to seek solutions. They focused on the three strikes they believed urban African Americans had against them at birth. The three strikes were the lack of care for mothers-to-be, inferior schools, and jobless parents. The leader of the group was Minister Louis Farrakhan (FAHR-uh-kahn). He decided to organize a march.

Farrakhan asked African American men to meet in Washington, DC, on October 16, 1995. The event was called the Million Man March.

Farrakhan wanted the men to come together to think about their responsibilities to themselves, their families, and their communities. The march's organizers also wanted to call attention to the problems African Americans faced. About 400,000 African American men attended the march.

African Americans have worked hard to break the color barriers that had long divided the country. They fought for civil rights, overcame obstacles, and lived out their dreams. African Americans have proven the importance of respecting the rights and freedoms of all human beings.

Minister Louis Farrakhan

Belief System

Farrakhan was a leader of the Nation of Islam. The Nation of Islam is a religion founded in 1930 in Detroit, Michigan. It follows some of the teachings of traditional Islam. But its members believe that the Nation of Islam's founder Wallace Fard Muhammad was Allah, or God, sent to Earth.

Fallen Leader

In the 1960s, African American leader Malcolm X was a popular Nation of Islam minister. He encouraged African Americans to use violence to get equal rights. He was assassinated in 1965.

The Million Man March in Washington, DC

Glossary

Academy Award—a yearly award given by the Academy of Motion Picture Arts and Sciences for outstanding achievement in film

aerospace engineering—the design, construction, and science of aircraft and spacecraft

affirmative action—an effort to improve the educational and employment opportunities of members of minority groups

columnist—a person who writes a regular feature in a newspaper or magazine

commentary—a form of writing in which the author comments on or gives opinions about a topic

diplomat—a person appointed to work on a country's political, economic, and social relations with other countries

discrimination—treatment based on race, class, or another category rather than individual merit

executive order—an order having the force of law issued by the president

expertise—expert skill or knowledge

gospel music—popular Christian church music with a strong rhythm

impartial—fair, unbiased

inauguration—induction into office

integrate—to unite into a whole

minority—a smaller group of people within a larger group

Nobel Prize—an international award given each year for outstanding achievement in physics, chemistry, medicine or physiology, literature, and the promotion of peace

ophthalmology—the branch of medicine that treats eye conditions

patent—an official government document given to an inventor to show ownership of a product or idea

pioneers—people who explore new areas of thought or activity

pop culture—short for popular culture; includes the music, movies, television shows, and celebrities that are popular at any given time

poverty—the state of not having enough money for basic needs

prejudices—unfair opinions formed without facts or evidence

Pulitzer Prize—yearly awards given for outstanding achievement in journalism, literature, and music

quotas—numbers or percentages that are the targeted minimums

rioted—having created a violent public disturbance

segregated—separated by race

unemployment—the state of not having a job

Index

Your Turn!

President John F. Kennedy first called for affirmative action in 1961. Affirmative action meant purposely creating opportunities for African Americans, women, and other minority groups. In 1965, President Lyndon B. Johnson issued an executive order to enforce affirmative action policies. These policies were very controversial.

Acting Out
Research three specific affirmative action policies in America's past. Choose one policy and write a play for that policy. The play should explain the policy in an interesting way.